Olympic Kate

by Sue Kendall

Olympic Kate

by Sue Kendall

Burlington Books
P. O. Box 54411
3721 Limassol
Cyprus
Burlington Books is an imprint of Danos Books Ltd.

Acknowledgement:

The publisher would like to thank the following people:

Castellano:	Blanca Mutlló Pàmies
Català:	Maria Esteve Serraviñals
Euskara:	Edurne Azkue Urrestilla
Galego:	Ramón Nicolás Rodríguez

ISBN 978-9963-47-568-1

Burlington Reader No. 4.23

10 9 8 7 6 5 4 3
16 15 14 13 12 11 10 09 08

TABLE OF CONTENTS

INTRODUCCIÓN

Desde que Kate Armstrong era niña ya soñaba con triunfar como gimnasta. Es en la adolescencia cuando le llega la oportunidad de ver su sueño realizado: representar a Gran Bretaña en los Juegos Olímpicos y ganar una medalla. A su mejor amiga, Becky, la seleccionan como sustituta en el equipo británico y las dos amigas entrenan duro para el gran día. Sin embargo, el sueño de Kate se ve truncado cuando no pasa el examen médico y da positivo en el control antidopaje. Se queda desconsolada pues es inocente de los cargos que recaen sobre ella. Su entrenador, Ben, cree en su inocencia e intenta demostrarlo con la ayuda del novio de Kate, Andrew. La policía se suma a la investigación y, tras preguntar a los sospechosos, el verdadero culpable confiesa. ¿Quién puede ser?

INTRODUCCIÓ

Des que la Kate Armstrong era una nena ja somiava amb triomfar com a gimnasta. A l'adolescència és quan li arriba l'oportunitat de veure realitzat el seu somni: representar la Gran Bretanya als Jocs Olímpics i guanyar una medalla. A la seva millor amiga, la Becky, la seleccionen com a substituta a l'equip britànic i les dues amigues entrenen intensament per al gran dia. No obstant això, el somni de la Kate es trenca quan no passa l'examen mèdic i dóna positiu en el control antidopatge. Es queda desconsolada perquè és innocent dels càrrecs que recauen sobre ella. El seu entrenador, en Ben, creu en la seva innocència i intenta demostrar-ho amb l'ajuda del xicot de la Kate, l'Andrew. La policia s'afegeix a la investigació i, després de preguntar als sospitosos, el verdader culpable confessa. Qui pot ser?

SARRERA

Kate Armstrongek umetatik zuen amets gimnasta bezala arrakasta izatea. Nerabezaroan etorriko zaio, ordea, ametsa gauzatzeko aukera: Joko Olinpikoetan Britainia Handiaren ordezkaria izatea eta domina bat irabaztea. Honen lagun minena, Becky, Britainiako taldean ordezkotzat aukeratu dute, eta bi lagunak gogor entrenatuko dira egun handirako. Dena den, Kateren ametsa zapuztu egingo da azterketa medikua ez gainditzean eta antidoping kontrolean baiezkoa ematean. Atsekabetuta dago, egozten dizkioten karguen erruduna ez baita. Entrenatzaileak, Benek, neskatoaren errugabetasunean sinesten du, eta Kateren mutil-laguna den Andrewen laguntzarekin, hori frogatzen saituko da. Poliziak ere ikerketarekin bat egingo du, eta susmagarri guztiei galderak egin ondoren, benetako errudunak aitortu egingo du. Nor izan daiteke?

LIMIAR

Dende que Kate Armstrong era nena xa soñaba con triunfar como ximnasta. É na adolescencia cando lle chega a oportunidade de ver o seu soño realizado: representar a Gran Bretaña nos Xogos Olímpicos e gañar unha medalla. Á súa mellor amiga, Becky, selecciónana como substituta no equipo británico e as dúas amigas adestran duro para o gran día. Porén, o soño de Kate vese truncado cando non pasa o exame médico e dá positivo no control antidopaxe. Queda desconsolada pois é inocente dos cargos que recaen sobre ela. O seu adestrador, Ben, cre na súa inocencia e intenta demostralo coa axuda do noivo de Kate, Andrew. A policía súmase á investigación e, logo de preguntar aos sospeitosos, o verdadeiro culpábel confesa. Quen pode ser?

Olympic Kate

CHAPTER 1 — The Life of an Athlete

My name is Kate Armstrong and I'm 17 years old. I've wanted to be a gymnast since I was a small child. I thought about it all the time. Mum says I'm lucky. Many people don't find their vocation in life until they're much older. Some people never find it.

An athlete's life isn't easy. I've got a very difficult routine. Every day I wake up at 4.00 am, have a good breakfast, and run to the sports centre on the other side of town. I **train** there for gymnastics **championships** with twenty other girls. Then, at 9.00 am, we go to school. When I get there, I try to concentrate on my lessons and not **fall asleep** during the long day.

At lunch, I don't eat hamburgers and chips from the canteen, like the rest of the class. I sit with Becky, my best friend and **team-mate**, and eat healthy, boring food. I've had to follow a special diet since my first day of **training** – fruit and vegetables, pasta for energy, and lots of milk and yoghurt. I mustn't eat food with too many calories, but I can eat more than some athletes, because I'm still young and my metabolism is good. This is the rule: you must eat healthy food and the portions must be small.

In the afternoon, I return to the sports centre to train for four more hours with our trainer, Ben. He is a great person, but he's very strict. We always work very hard and he thinks we've got a good chance to compete in the Olympics.

After training, I go home and have another healthy meal. Then I go to my room, do my homework and go to sleep, exhausted. The next day I start the entire routine again. This is how it's been since I was ten years old.

I've always envied my younger brother, Tom. I come home, and he's already sitting in front of the TV or playing on his computer.

All this is hard for me sometimes. But the worst part is my social life – it's almost non-existent! Over the past few years, I've had very little time to be with my friends. To be honest, last year I decided I was tired of this life. Our team was chosen to be in the national competition and the extra hours of training were very difficult for me. I wanted to stop gymnastics and to be an **ordinary teenager** again – go out for pizza with friends, stay out late on Saturday nights, sleep till lunchtime on Sundays like the other kids in my class. I wanted a normal teenage life. I decided to tell my parents about it.

Then I met Andrew. Andrew is two years older than I am. We train at the same gym, at the sports centre. We both love sports but we've also got a lot of other things in common. We enjoy the same films, love animals, and want to travel around the world.

One day, Andrew surprised me. "There's a new film at the cinema," he said. "I've heard it's really funny. Do you want to go with me? It's at 10.00 on Saturday night."

"Do you want to go to the cinema with me?" Andrew asked.

At that moment, I didn't think at all about my training. "Sure! That sounds good," I answered immediately.

When I got home and told my parents, they were very angry.

"How can you **go on a date** with this boy?" Dad asked. "You don't know anything about him or his family."

"Yes, I do," I answered. "Andrew lives at home with his parents and three sisters. He's studying **law** at university, and he's doing his training at a lawyer's office in town."

"Hmm … " was Dad's answer. What could he say?

"But how can you stay out late at the weekend?" asked Mum. "That's your only time for relaxation. You have to be at training at 5.00 am on Monday."

I was very unhappy, but I tried not to **let it show**. "I've spoken to Andrew several times at the gym. He's a great guy," I said. "And I need other things in my life at the weekend, not just sleep. I also need to have *fun*." I was almost crying then.

My parents were silent. After a few minutes, my mother said, "Well, let us meet Andrew first. If he's as wonderful as you say he is, I'm sure we'll like him."

Andrew came to my house the following day. I was very nervous, but he was calm. "Relax, Kate. Everything's going to be fine," he said patiently.

Andrew was right. My parents asked him a lot of questions, but that didn't frighten him. He answered every one.

In the end, my parents liked Andrew. They let me go to a film with him. But before we left the house, they had a long conversation with us. Andrew had to hear about how important my training sessions are and how important it is to rest before I start a new week of training sessions.

Since then Andrew and I have been together a lot – except for all my hours of training. We talk on the phone when we can and we usually meet on Saturdays and Sundays. Andrew convinced me to continue with my training and to try to get to the Olympics.

CHAPTER 2 PREPARING FOR THE OLYMPICS

Before we went to the World Championships, I had to answer a school questionnaire. One of the questions was: "What is your ambition in life?" What could I write? I thought about my answer for a few minutes. For years, my ambition was to be in the **winning** team of the British Schools Gymnastics Championships. But in April that dream became a reality! Our gymnastics team won the British Women's Team Championship for seniors.

The competition was in a place called Guildford, and it was very **exciting**. We were great! We were much better than the other teams. And now we wanted to go to the Olympics and win a medal there. The question was this: Could we make our dream a reality? Suddenly, I knew the answer and I wrote it on the questionnaire: "My ambition is to win a gold medal at the Olympics."

The next few months after the competition were quite hard. I've never felt so stressed before. If we wanted to send a full team of six to the Olympics, we had to finish in the **top** 12 teams at the World Championships. This was not going to be easy.

The World Championships were in October. The competitors included the top 10 countries from the previous Olympics, and several teams from the **host** country of the next Olympics. Some of the other teams were strong like ours. They were the best from their countries. But the number one team was the French one. We were very good, but they were better than us. Their best gymnast was a girl called Estelle Lorraine. It was incredible to watch her because she did every exercise perfectly. In the end, the French team won the World Championships and we were second. In my opinion, they won because of Estelle. After the competition, I saw Estelle leaving the gym and I decided to approach her.

"You were wonderful, Estelle," I said. "You're a very talented gymnast."

"I know," she answered, and walked out of the gym with her nose in the air.

I was surprised. "She's very arrogant," I thought. "It doesn't cost anything to say 'thank you'." I didn't like her very much.

Estelle walked out of the gym with her nose in the air.

Even though we didn't win the World Championships, our team could still send a full team of six gymnasts to the Olympics. When we returned home, we began to compete for these six places. There were 13 of us in the team and we all wanted to take part in the Olympics. It wasn't going to be easy. I practised for several days with Ben, our trainer. I had to do better than **at least** seven other girls, but I wanted to be the best.

One Friday at 12.00, Ben was going to announce the names of the girls in the Olympic team. I was so nervous. I couldn't eat all morning. I just sat in my room and waited. Andrew called.

"Phone me **as soon as** you know something – good or bad," he said.

"OK," I answered.

I got to the sports centre an hour early. At exactly 12.00, Ben read the list very slowly. I wasn't first. I wasn't second. But then I heard my name: "And number three is Kate Armstrong," Ben announced. I was so excited.

Ben continued to read the other names. Becky wasn't on the list. I felt so sad for her. Then he added, "And now for the substitute gymnasts. There'll be two of you. If one of the other gymnasts can't compete for some reason, you'll compete **instead**." His next words were: "Becky Walters". I was euphoric. My friend Becky was going too! But she wasn't very happy because she wasn't in the first team.

"Becky, you're going to the Olympics! *That's* the most important thing," I said. "*We're* going to the Olympics. Let's hope you'll have an opportunity to be in the team in the end." Becky felt a little better. Then we both got very excited and started to make plans.

Becky and I have been good friends for a long time but there's always been some competition between us. I suppose that's natural. She's a little envious of me because I usually get higher **scores** than she does. But I adore her and our friendship is a lot more important to me than sport. I often tell her that, because it's how I really feel. I think she knows it.

It's hard to believe, but since the team was chosen for the Olympics, our training sessions were even longer and more difficult than usual. Our school gave us extra time to practise. We left classes at 2.00 pm and practised at the gym for six hours every day. Ben added Saturday as an extra training day, so I had less time to be with Andrew.

Our training sessions have become even longer and more difficult than usual.

Andrew **didn't complain**, but it wasn't easy for him **either**. He knew how important this was to me, so he tried to be as helpful as possible. He always drove me home after training. And he knew when to go home and let me sleep so I could wake up in time for training the next morning.

♦ ♦ ♦

In January, our team went to train at the National Sports Centre in Lilleshall, a village in Shropshire, near the border of Wales. We were going to be in training there for six months. It's a great honour to train at Lilleshall. It was once the home of the Duke of Sutherland, and Britain's top sportsmen and women train there in all kinds of sports, especially for the Olympics. It has got some of the best gymnastics equipment in the world. And it's the best place for teams to **focus** on their sports, because it's quiet and far from any big cities. There are beautiful gardens all around and the atmosphere is very tranquil.

Andrew and I had a long conversation before I left. "This will be a difficult time for you, Kate. I know that," he said. "But don't worry. You'll do well because you've trained a lot and you **care** so much. I'll think about you all the time. Just remember that and try not to feel sad."

"How did I find a boyfriend like Andrew? He's one in a million!" I thought to myself. "I'm so lucky." Then I said to him, "The Olympics are very important to me. But if we win, I'll be ready to leave the team and travel around the world with you."

It was quite possible for our team to win at least one medal. If we didn't get the gold, then we might win a silver or bronze medal. Our team was one of the best. Andrew knew that too, so he said, "You may not want to leave sport after the excitement of the Olympics, Kate. And if you win, your life will change a lot. There may not be a place for me in your life then."

"No, that's not true," I answered. "You'll always be more important to me." But I don't know if he really believed me.

CHAPTER 3 TRAINING CAMP

I came home from Lilleshall at the end of June and spent two weeks with my family. That was before I left for the final training camp. It was great to be back at home. We didn't do anything special, just the usual things – we walked in the park, met friends, went to the cinema. In the evenings, Andrew came to visit and we all sat and talked and laughed together. My parents began to like Andrew even more than they did before. We all remembered my first date with him, and how they interrogated him before we went out. We laughed about it.

Soon it was time for me to go to our final training camp in Belarus and I was really excited. I knew almost nothing about the place, except that athletes trained there for the 2000 Olympics in Sydney. Before I left, I read about Belarus on the Internet. Belarus is one of the Eastern European countries and its capital city is called Minsk. At different times in history it was part of Lithuania, Poland and finally the Soviet Union. Then, in 1991, it became an independent country.

Belarus can be **cool**, even in the summer. It's a beautiful country, with many lakes, rivers and forests, but we only saw a little of the place through the window of the bus on our way from the airport. From the day we arrived, we began our training.

At the training camp in Belarus, we could train without any interruptions from family and friends, so it was much easier to concentrate. It was a little lonely sometimes, but Becky and I were in the same room and that helped a lot.

The camp wasn't as nice as the one in Lilleshall. The gym was a little smaller than the one there, so we had to train as efficiently as possible. At 8.00 am we ran for twenty minutes and then came back and fought to be first **in line** to shower. Then we had breakfast, and returned to the gym to train until 1.30 pm. After lunch, we walked to the arena across the road to do full competition **routines**. At 8.00 pm we returned for dinner and then went to bed till the next morning.

At 8.00 am we ran for 20 minutes.

Ben and the rest of the British Olympic trainers worked very hard with us, both as a group and as individuals. I made a lot of progress at the training camp and learned a few interesting things about myself in the process.

I discovered that my ideas about myself changed a lot. Sometimes I felt like I was the best in the world, and other times I felt I was the worst. The reality is usually somewhere in the middle, so I needed somebody to give me **advice**. My family wasn't there, so I depended on Ben for that. He and the other trainers gave all of us a lot of emotional **support**.

The time at the training camp also helped me to understand the other girls better. We **shared** our secrets and comforted one another in times of need. We learned to identify our own difficulties and help each other **succeed**. This is important, because my real family has always been there to help me, but during the Olympics I won't be permitted to contact them. The girls in the team are my family now and I hope we'll always be friends and not let the Olympics change our friendships.

CHAPTER 4 A Party at the Olympics

I can't believe how quickly the time has passed since the training camp in Belarus ended. Now I'm sitting in my room at the **hall of residence** – waiting for the Olympic Games to begin. This is the most important week in my gymnastics career, probably in my entire life. I miss Andrew a lot. Ben has taken our mobile phones because we need to concentrate only on the competition. I'm not in contact with Andrew, but I know he's in the city somewhere, waiting for the big day, like all of us. Mum and Dad are also in the city. They're staying at a hotel near the Olympic Village. It's hard to be away from everyone – I depend so much on their love and support. But I'm lucky because Becky is here with me.

I've spoken to many of the girls from the other teams since I arrived here. We've got a lot in common. It's also exciting to learn about life in other countries. We're all going to compete against each other in a few days, but we're still friendly, except for Estelle Lorraine, the arrogant French girl. She's my greatest rival and I really don't like her. She always talks about how important it is to get a gold medal. She'll do anything to win.

Tomorrow morning a few of us are having a medical examination. We're going to be tested by the Olympic doctors to see if we've taken drugs to help us do better in the competitions. Ben isn't permitted to accompany me to the examination because he's a male, so Hilary, one of the female trainers, will go in his place. I don't mind, because I know Hilary and I feel comfortable with her.

Suddenly, Becky comes into the room. "The girls on our floor are going up to the **roof** for a few hours," she says. "One of the girls in the French team has convinced the guard to give us the key. Do you want to come?"

"I don't know," I answer. "I don't think so. I prefer to go to bed early."

But Becky really wants to go. "Please come. It'll be fun," she says. "And we all need to relax a little before the competition." In the end, she convinces me.

"OK, I'll go with you, but only for a short time," I tell her.

"Thanks, Kate. You're the best!" says Becky. "Go up to the roof. I'll be there in a minute."

I go to the roof alone and I'm surprised to see some of the girls drinking alcohol there. How can they do that the night before the medical examination? An athlete shouldn't drink alcohol under normal circumstances. But during the week of the Olympics! I just don't understand it.

Becky soon comes up to the roof with two big bottles of water, one for each of us. "Take this," she says. "Don't let anybody convince you to drink alcohol."

"How can these girls drink alcohol?" I ask.

"Hilary once explained it to me," answers Becky. "There are two kinds of athletes – Olympians and Olympic tourists. The

Olympians are here to win. But the other athletes, the Olympic tourists, will never win and they know that. They're just here for the experience – it's obvious."

"So they don't care if they can't compete?" I ask.

"That's right," answers Becky.

We decide to stay on the roof for half an hour just to be sociable, and then we plan to 'disappear'.

Suddenly, Estelle takes out her mobile phone and starts to talk quietly to somebody. "She's lucky. Her trainer lets her and the other girls in the French team keep their mobile phones and talk to anybody they want to," I think to myself. "Maybe Estelle's talking to Mimi, the girl from her room. I don't think Mimi is here **yet**. She's as ambitious as Estelle, and not very pleasant. I hope she won't come and ruin this evening."

Half an hour later, we're still on the roof. Becky tells us stupid Olympic **jokes** and soon we're all laughing hysterically. I'm starting to enjoy myself, **releasing** some of the tension caused by the intensive training.

Estelle is sitting very quietly on the side. This is strange, since she usually likes being the centre of attention. Then Estelle's trainer, Monique, comes and sits beside her. "Maybe she's going to tell Estelle to leave," I think to myself. Monique talks to Estelle for a few minutes. Then I think, "Estelle is probably just worried about the competition and Monique is trying to calm her." But to my surprise, Monique gets up and comes to sit beside me. She talks about how beautiful it is in the Olympic Village and how exciting it is to be here.

"So, what do you think, Kate?" she asks. "Is your team going to win?"

She seems to be trying to get information from Estelle's competitors and I answer her politely. I'm happy because she obviously sees me as one of Estelle's greatest rivals. Then, she continues to sit beside me for about ten minutes. "She's only doing this to be nice," I think to myself. Soon I forget about her and enjoy Becky's jokes. She's very funny tonight.

Monique seems to be trying to get information.

Becky and I stay for an hour and then I begin to feel a little ill, so we return to our room. By 10.30 pm, I'm feeling very ill, so I get into bed. "It's just nerves," says Becky. I need some medicine, but I don't take anything because I don't want it to affect my medical examination the next day.

CHAPTER 5 The Medical Examination

Hilary comes at 7.30 am to take a few of us to the medical examination. I'm feeling better now, even though I slept very badly during the night. Usually, only the best competitors are tested. That's probably why some of the girls drank alcohol last night. But a few others are often selected too.

Hilary explains the drug-testing process to us. Then she fills in the forms, giving details of all our medication, vitamins and food supplements. During our training, Ben and the other trainers give us supplements to make us stronger and better gymnasts. It's all legal, so there's no problem.

I sit for half an hour until they call my name. I'm the last one in line. I've done this before so usually I don't worry very much. But this is the Olympics! I enter the room and Hilary goes with me. She must be present in case there are any problems. There are more doctors than usual and everyone is serious. One of them looks at my form, reads it carefully, and signs it. Then a nurse takes some blood from me and gives me permission to go.

We leave the room and I immediately feel calmer. I soon forget about the examination. We all have breakfast with Ben before training starts at 9.00 am as usual.

At breakfast, Ben talks about the last few days of training. "These days are crucial for all of us," he says. "You must concentrate only on your training – nothing else. I'll worry about the rest." At the end, he explains about the medical examination. "We'll get the results of the blood tests in the afternoon. But I'm sure everything will be fine, so let's have a good practice. We haven't got much time before the Olympics."

Suddenly, I feel very nervous. It's hard to believe, but the Olympics are in just a few days. I've missed a lot of fun times with other teenagers to get to this point in my career. Our trainers have worked so hard with us for years, and our families have given us their support. Now we must **do our best** for everyone – for ourselves, our families, our trainers and our team. But this time it's different. We've got an enormous responsibility – we represent not just our town or region, but our entire country! I feel good about our team. We've got a lot of team spirit and I know we'll do well.

We return to the gym. While I'm waiting to go on the bars, I see Estelle for a few seconds. She's training in the next room and the door is half open. Her routine is very complicated, but as always, she does each exercise perfectly and elegantly. It's going to be a very difficult competition and I try not to worry. I start thinking about Andrew and our plans for the future. I imagine us travelling everywhere – first to Europe, then to the Far East and from there to North and South America. There's so much to see. I think about it and I automatically start to feel better.

In the end, the morning practice goes well and Ben is satisfied. At 12.00 he takes us for a big, healthy lunch. Then he says, "Go to your rooms now and relax. I'll tell you the results of the blood tests as soon as I get them."

Becky and I return to our room. We sit and talk. "I know I won't compete in the end," Becky says sadly. "Everybody is fine and I'm happy about that. But I probably won't have an opportunity to participate. It's very frustrating."

I try to help her see the positive side. "Look, Becky," I say, "The Olympics is the most important sports competition in the world and you're here. You should be happy, even if you don't compete in the end."

"I know, I know," Becky answers. "But still … "

I haven't got **anything left** to say, so I go and lie on my bed. I think about the last few days – so much has happened – and then I fall asleep.

In my sleep I see my team standing with me on the winners' podium. We've each got a gold medal around our necks and everybody is smiling at us. Becky is there too. Suddenly, I'm woken by a loud sound. Somebody is at the door.

CHAPTER 6 BAD NEWS

I open the door and Ben is standing there, in front of me. He looks very serious. "Come and talk to me in the entrance hall. I've got something very important to tell you," he says. "I'll wait for you there."

I wash my face and **comb** my hair. Then I look at the clock. It's 3.30 pm. "What can be wrong?" I think. "Why did Ben look so worried?" My first thought is about Andrew and my parents, of course. Something has happened to one of them. I'm sure of it. I get to the entrance hall and Ben is waiting for me.

"Are my parents and Andrew all right?" I ask Ben.

"They're all fine, Kate. I spoke to them an hour ago," he says. Then he waits a few seconds and says slowly, "That's not the problem, I'm afraid."

At first, I relax a little. And then I begin to worry again. "Then, what *is* the problem? What can be so terrible?" I ask.

Ben is very uncomfortable. He doesn't talk immediately. Finally, he says, "I don't know how to say this, Kate, especially to you. You've always played by the rules. But I want to be completely honest with you and please do the same with me. If you tell me the truth, I promise to give you all my support. I just can't understand how this can be."

"What are you talking about, Ben? What's wrong?" I ask, totally confused.

Then Ben takes out a piece of paper. It looks very official. He waits a moment before he begins. "According to the blood test from this morning, you had some drugs in your body. You can't participate in the Olympics, Kate."

He stops and looks at me to see my reaction.

"You can't participate in the Olympics, Kate," said Ben.

I don't move. I'm surprised. I don't understand this. I've never taken drugs in my life.

Ben continues. "I'm sure this is a terrible mistake. Maybe you took some unconventional food supplements, or something to help you control your nerves. Try to think, Kate. It's very important. Did anybody give you anything?"

I think for a few seconds. Did I take anything different yesterday? No, just the usual supplements. Maybe there was something in the food at the Olympic cafeteria. No, that's ridiculous. Everybody has lunch there. Did I eat something on the roof last night? No, I just drank some water. So I say to Ben, "Ben, the most important thing in my life right now is the Olympics. I would never do that. And I never take medicines. I've never needed them. And I know how important it is to keep my body healthy. This is all a mystery to me."

Ben looks at me attentively while I'm talking and then he says, "I believe you, Kate. You've always been an honest girl. But we've got to understand the cause of this. Please tell me everything – and I mean everything. What have you done since the end of training yesterday?"

I feel very uncomfortable. I'm not happy about the party on the roof last night and now I feel even worse because I don't want to tell Ben about it. But I must. He has to know everything. So I explain things to him.

"Becky came into the room … " I start. At first I don't mention the girls and the alcohol, but in the end, I tell him about it. I don't hide anything.

"Maybe you drank some alcohol by mistake," he says. "And maybe something happened **afterwards** and you didn't know."

"No, it didn't happen like that," I insist. "I don't even like alcohol. Becky brought two bottles of water for us to drink. I forgot to mention that."

"So did Becky stay on the roof, too?" Ben asks.

"Yes. But she didn't drink any alcohol, only water," I answer. "And she returned to the room with me after an hour. I went to bed at 10.30 pm." I hope Ben won't get angry with Becky. I feel terrible because she didn't do anything bad. She was trying to help me.

Ben listens to me very carefully and then he says, "It's OK, Kate. Don't worry. You haven't done anything wrong, I'm sure. I've got confidence in you. I'll discover the truth."

"Am I really **disqualified** from the competition?" I ask very quietly.

"Yes, Kate," Ben answers sadly. "But I'll do absolutely everything to solve this mystery. There's something wrong here and I'm going to get to the bottom of it. Trust me."

I don't listen to Ben after the first sentence. How can this be true? "I've trained for so many years and now I can't participate in the Olympics because of something so incredible, so **unfair**,"

I think to myself. "This isn't happening! I don't believe it!"

Ben sees the worry in my eyes. He feels sorry for me. "Listen, Kate. Please go to your room now," he tells me. "Stay with Becky and relax for a while. Try not to think about this. I'll do my best to help you. I'll return in a few hours and tell you if I've discovered anything. If you think of anything new, go and tell Hilary. She'll call me."

CHAPTER 7 A Conversation with Andrew

I get to my room and open the door. Becky is sitting on her bed and I tell her the bad news. "This is so unfair. How could I test positive for drugs?" I protest.

"What are you talking about?" says Becky. "I'm sure there's a logical explanation for this. Maybe they confused your test with somebody else's," she tries to console me. "It's probably all a big mistake. Don't worry, Kate. Everything will be fine."

It's good to hear these words from Becky, but she can't guarantee anything. We both know that.

"You're probably right," I answer. "I've always been careful to obey all the rules. I try not to make any mistakes. Drugs aren't a problem, because they've never interested me. They're so destructive. I don't know how anybody can use them, especially athletes."

"I agree with you," answers Becky. "Listen, Kate, just lie down and rest for a while. Ben will return soon with good news. You'll see."

Suddenly, I say something very stupid. I'm nervous and I don't think before I speak.

"Well, Becky, your opportunity is finally here," I announce. "Now you'll get to participate in the Olympics in my place."

Becky looks at me as if I've just hit her. She walks back a few steps and just stands there, looking very hurt. I want to **take back** my words immediately, but it's too late.

"Is that your opinion of me – your best friend?" she finally says. "I've never even considered the possibility. I know how important it is to you to participate in the Olympics. I'm ready to go home right now if that can help you!" She starts to cry and I do too. I cry enough tears to fill a swimming pool.

"Is that your opinion of me – your best friend?" Becky finally says.

"Oh, Becky, I'm sorry," I tell her. "I don't know why I said that. You *are* my best friend and you've been so good to me. I shouldn't say such things. I'm just so disappointed."

"I know, I know," says Becky, crying. She puts her arms around me. "It's OK. I know you didn't mean it," she says again and again.

"I should go and lie down before any other stupid things come out of my mouth," I say after a few minutes. So I lie down and try to relax. It's impossible for me to sleep, of course. I think of Andrew. He always helps me to think rationally. But I can't call him because I haven't got a mobile phone. So I just lie in bed and cry. And then suddenly I remember Estelle. She's got a mobile. Her trainer lets her use it. She definitely isn't my best friend but at a time like this she might help me. I wash my face and comb my hair. She mustn't see how bad I'm feeling.

I arrive at Estelle's room and **knock on** the door.

"Come in. It's open," says a voice from inside.

I open the door slowly and see Estelle sitting on her bed, reading a sports magazine. She looks at me strangely. I try to smile but she doesn't smile back.

"Hi, Estelle. How are you?" I begin. "I see they finally gave you a chance to relax a little. That's a great magazine. I read it every month. It's got some very good articles on gymnastics."

I seem really stupid. I just talk and talk and I don't think. Estelle looks at me for a minute. "What do you want?" she finally asks, in her French accent.

"I need to use your phone to call my boyfriend," I answer. "It's an emergency! You see, Ben, our trainer, took our phones. He won't let us talk to anybody at the Olympics." I'm silent as I wait for a few, very long seconds.

Estelle looks at me suspiciously and then she says, "OK. It's on the table **over there**." She shows me the table in the corner of the room.

I can't believe it. She doesn't even ask me about the emergency. Maybe she's nicer than I think she is. I don't give her time to **change her mind**. I go to the table and take the phone.

"I'll pay you for the call," I say.

"Don't worry about it," she answers.

I go into the **hall** and find a private place to sit. I call Andrew's mobile phone and it rings four times. Finally, he answers.

"Hello. Who is this?" Andrew asks. He, of course, doesn't

recognise the number.

"It's me, Kate. Oh, Andrew. I'm so glad to hear your voice." I almost start to cry, but I stop myself.

"What's wrong, Kate? Why are you calling me? Why aren't you in training?"

"It's a long story, Andrew. You won't believe it."

"Tell me, I've always got time for you."

"What's wrong Kate? Why aren't you in training?" Andrew asks.

So I tell him everything, from the beginning. Andrew is studying to be a lawyer, so he asks me all kinds of questions. I tell him more than I told Ben, because his questions help me remember more details. "I went to bed at 10.30 pm because I was feeling very ill," I finish. He doesn't say anything for a few seconds.

"Listen to me, Kate. This is very strange. Somebody is trying to hurt you," Andrew tells me. "Ben has got a lot of experience. You must have confidence in him. He'll help you and in the end you'll participate in the games. You'll see. Just wait patiently until he returns."

"There's nothing else I can do, I guess. It's just so good to hear your voice. It calms me."

"Don't worry, Kate. We'll always be together."

"OK, Andrew. Thanks. I have to go now." **By this time** I'm really crying, but I can't let Andrew hear me.

I sit in the hall for a few minutes and then return to Estelle's room. She's still reading the magazine. I enter the room and she looks up for a second. I give her the phone.

"Thanks, Estelle," I say.

"That's OK," she says and she continues reading her magazine.

"What a strange girl," I think to myself. "I can't understand her at all."

But I've got more important things to think about. I return to my room and sit on my bed, waiting for Ben. Maybe he'll have some news.

CHAPTER 8 SUSPICIONS

Ben finally arrives at the hall of residence with an **official** from the Olympic committee and two policemen. "Are they going to arrest me?" I think to myself. "Am I going to stay in prison tonight?" I begin to panic, but the police and the official pass my door.

Ben stops to talk to me. "Wait here with Becky, Kate," he says. "I'll return soon and tell you if there's any news."

I sit on my bed in my room, feeling very perturbed. I start complaining to poor Becky again.

"Why is this happening to me? I've never done anything wrong in my life. I've never even crossed the street at a red light. All I've ever wanted is to be the best at gymnastics. I've never tried to hurt anybody. And now the police want to arrest me. I don't even know anything about drugs."

"I know, Kate," says Becky. "I'm sure everything will be all right. Try to be patient."

I can't think of a rational explanation. Maybe Ben gave me the drugs and I didn't know. He's always giving me all these health drinks. Some trainers do terrible things to their gymnasts to help them win. Could Ben be one of them?

But then I think again. Ben knew about the medical examination. They had to find the drugs in my blood. But maybe in his opinion the drugs weren't going to show in my blood. Is that possible? And what about the rest of the girls? They took the same supplements. They ate the same food. I'm so confused. In any case, I can't do anything about it now.

Half an hour later, I hear a noise outside my room. I open the door and look into the hall. I see Ben, the official, and the policemen. They're walking in my direction. My heart **is beating** very fast.

Ben calls Becky to come out and talk to the policemen and the official. A few minutes later, she leaves with Ben and the policemen. Then I see Estelle. She looks very angry and she's waiting for them near the entrance.

"She'll probably tell them about my phone call to Andrew," I think. "Oh, no! Now Andrew will be in **trouble** too, all because of me."

And then I think, "What about Estelle? Maybe she's responsible for my situation. It's definitely a possibility. She always has to be the best. 'I'll do anything to win,' I've heard her say on more than one occasion."

I sit in my room alone and frightened, and I wait. "This is the worst moment in my life," I think to myself.

Finally, after about an hour, Ben returns. I look at him suspiciously. Has he got more bad news? We sit down in the hall and he begins to talk.

"Everything's going to be fine," he says. "Try to relax. You'll just have to take another test tomorrow and if the results are OK, you can participate in the competition."

Becky leaves with Ben and the policemen.

"But what has happened?" I ask.

Ben explains, "I spoke to the doctors. They've discovered a certain drug in your body. From their experience, this drug only stays in the blood for a short time, unless it is taken regularly. The amount of drugs in your body was very small. It entered your body only last night. And last night you didn't take any drugs at all, right?" he asks again, just to be sure.

"Oh, Ben, how can you ask me that?" I answer. "I'm not that kind of person. You know that. Maybe the supplements have affected me in a negative way. What do you think? Is it possible?"

He looks at me strangely for a moment and then he says, "No, of course not. I could never do anything to hurt your opportunities at the Olympics. It's very important for me too, you know."

And again he explains, "The drugs in your body were from last night, not from before."

"Is he telling me the truth?" I ask myself. I'm so paranoid. I can't think logically any more.

Then Ben says, "Look, Kate, I've got one more question to ask you."

"Ben, I've already told you that I don't use drugs! And I'm very offended. Please don't ask me again."

"No, no. Listen to me, Kate. I didn't want to ask you that. I only want to know one thing. Did Becky maybe put the drugs in your water?"

I'm surprised. That possibility has never occurred to me. "Oh no, definitely not!" I answer, but I'm not really sure at all.

I start to think again. It was Becky's idea to go onto the roof last night, but we didn't go up there together. She brought the water after I was already there and she was talking all the time. That's why I didn't notice anything strange around me. And, worst of all, Becky really wants to be in the Olympics and she can only participate if somebody else doesn't. But, no! She's my best friend. She loves me. She couldn't do that.

"I know it's hard to accept," says Ben, "but we have to examine all the possibilities. Did she give you anything?" he asks cautiously. "Maybe you weren't looking and she put something in your water."

"I just don't know any more," I answer, desperately.

Suddenly Ben's mobile phone rings. It's Andrew. He's at the police station. Andrew talked to Ben immediately after I called him, I soon discover. He's trying to do his best to help. According to Andrew, the police have arrested Estelle and her trainer, Monique. They've also decided to keep Becky for a while, just to be sure.

I probably will participate in the Olympics, but I feel horrible. My rival is in prison. My best friend is in prison too! I don't believe anybody right now. I just want to go home.

CHAPTER 9 — Everything Becomes Clear

I don't know how I'm going to survive the next few hours. My mind is working all the time. It's filled with so many questions: Why does somebody want to hurt me? Is it Estelle? Is it her trainer? Maybe it's both of them. Can it be Becky, my best friend? Is she ready to do *anything* to participate in the Olympics? Maybe Ben is trying to protect himself. And then maybe it's somebody else.

I don't leave my room all evening. I don't talk to anybody. I try to come to some conclusions, but this only brings new questions: What if there are still drugs in my body and I don't pass the test tomorrow? Is this how my sports career is going to end? Will I even have the opportunity to participate in the Olympics?

Then I remember Andrew's words. "Don't worry," he said. "We'll always be together." And so I think, "That's true. We're still young. I can do other things and succeed at them too. In the end, an Olympic medal is not the most important thing in life. I got here and that's the main thing." I feel calmer now.

Finally, at around 9.00 pm, Ben returns. I look at him and try to read his mind. Is the news good or bad? I start to panic again.

Then he explains. "The police have discovered a residue of drugs in Monique's room and she has confessed. She put the drugs in your water while you were listening to Becky's stories. She did it because you are Estelle's greatest rival."

"Monique did it because you are Estelle's greatest rival," said Ben.

"Well, that's a compliment, I guess. Was Estelle **aware** of Monique's intentions?" I ask.

"No. According to Estelle, Monique wanted to meet you, so Estelle invited her to come up to the roof. Monique really intended to talk to *you*, but she didn't want it to be obvious, so she spoke to Estelle for a few minutes first. Estelle didn't know about her real intentions."

"And what about Becky?" I ask, a little frightened to hear the answer.

"Well, at first it looked like Becky was an accomplice.

She brought you water. Then she was talking all the time. This distracted you and you didn't see Monique put the drugs in your water. But in the end Monique has told the truth. Becky is innocent. She had nothing to do with it."

"Oh, I'm so happy to hear that." I begin to cry again.

"Well, Kate, all you have to do now is sleep well tonight. Tomorrow you'll have to take the blood test again – I'm sure it will be fine – and then you'll have to start training again, young lady."

"Ben, there's something I have to tell you," I begin slowly.

Ben tries to stop me. "You don't need to say anything."

"No, I insist," I begin. "I don't know how to say this exactly. I suspected you for a few hours today, Ben. I was very confused. I couldn't understand how I got into this situation. I wanted to accuse everyone. I'm very sorry, Ben. You've been a wonderful trainer – **sensitive** and considerate. And all this time you've tried to help me."

"It's OK, Kate. You've been under terrible pressure. It looked like your career was finished. I understand. I'm not angry. Believe me."

Again I start to cry. This is becoming a habit.

"Now, stay here and relax. Becky will return very soon. And Hilary will come for you at 7.30 am tomorrow for the test."

"OK, Ben. And thanks again."

Soon after Ben leaves, Becky arrives. She's very agitated. Now it's my turn to console her.

"Oh, Kate, it was terrible. I felt like a criminal."

"Becky, I'm so sorry. You were just trying to be a good friend. You're the best friend in the world. I'll never, never doubt you again."

"OK. I forgive you, Kate," says Becky.

I have to talk to one more person and that is Estelle. I don't like her very much, but I still feel bad because I suspected her.

I see her returning ten minutes later and I follow her to her room. She turns around and looks at me very strangely. I start to talk immediately.

"Estelle, I have to tell you the truth. In my mind, I accused you, and I'm sorry," I confess.

"In my mind, I accused you, and I'm sorry," I confess.

Her answer surprises me.

"No, Kate. *I'm* sorry," she says. "I really didn't know about Monique's plans. She was very wrong. If I'm going to win, it must be because I'm the best. It can't be because somebody **tricked** my opponent."

"Oh, Estelle, I'm so happy," I tell her. "I respect you very much. You're a great gymnast and it will be an honour to compete against you."

"I feel the same way," Estelle says. "You probably won't believe this, but I've admired you ever since we met at the World

Championships."

"Thanks. That's a big compliment," I say. "Estelle, can I ask you a favour?"

"Sure," she answers.

"Can I please use your phone one more time?" I ask, smiling. "It'll be the last time, I promise. I must call my boyfriend and thank him for his help."

Estelle laughs. I've never heard her laugh before. It's great.

"Of course," she answers, and she gives me her mobile.

I run to my private place in the hall and phone Andrew. This time he recognises the number.

"Hi, Kate. How are you?" he asks.

"I'm much better, thanks to you," I answer. "You don't know how much you helped me today."

"I really didn't do anything," says Andrew.

"You did more than you'll ever know. I'll see you soon and then I'll tell you," I say.

"OK, Kate. You should sleep now. Save your energy for the hardest part," Andrew tells me.

"OK, Andrew. I won't speak to you again until after the competitions, so wish me luck," I say.

"Good luck! Your parents and I will be sitting in the stadium and watching you. Just think of us and you'll be fine," he says.

"I will. Good night, Andrew," I say.

"Good night, Kate," says Andrew.

CHAPTER 10 THE OPENING CEREMONY

The next day I pass the medical examination without any trouble and I return to my training. It's great to have my passion in life back. I'm filled with energy and am feeling very confident. The girls in my team are very positive. My personal routines for the individual gymnastics competition are going extremely well and I hope to win a medal for that, too.

The first day of the Olympics finally arrives. All the

delegations are dressed in the colours of their countries. We're standing outside the Olympic stadium, waiting to enter. We watch the opening ceremony on an enormous screen.

The ceremony begins with a beautiful dance. Thousands of young people participate. They're wearing the national **costume** of the host country. The dance represents all the different aspects of the country's culture and history. It's spectacular. Not one person makes a mistake. They've practised this dance for a year, because it has to be perfect. Millions of people around the world are watching it on television. The audience applauds very loudly at the end of the dance. Then, the five Olympic rings are lit in a very big pool of water in the middle of the stadium. It's incredible to see.

In the **Parade** of Nations, all the delegations take part in the ceremony, and it starts after the **performance**. More than 10,500 of us athletes enter the stadium. Our leaders walk in first, carrying the flags of each country, and we follow them. More than 200 flags fill the stadium with colour.

The delegations enter the stadium in alphabetical order. We represent Great Britain and Northern Ireland, so we have to wait a long time before we can **join** the parade. I see Estelle walk in near the front of the French delegation. The audience applauds loudly every time a new country appears.

Soon, we are next in line. We're a large group, almost 300 sportsmen and women. Our country is the only one to send delegations to the Olympics every summer and winter since the start of the Olympics. This year we're competing in 22 different kinds of sports during the two weeks of the games.

The trainers are positioned at the front of our delegation. Ben is one of them. He's very proud and filled with enthusiasm. I can see it in the way he walks. The leader of the delegation is carrying the British flag, the Union Jack. As we pass, the British people in the audience stand and applaud. They're all moving their flags excitedly in the air. I begin to cry. Becky is walking next to me. I turn to look at her and she's crying too.

As we pass, the British people in the audience stand and applaud.

Becky takes my hand and looks directly at me. "This is the best day of my entire life," she says quietly. "Can you believe we're actually at the Olympics?"

"No, I can't," I answer. "It's like a dream, and I'm so happy you're a part of it."

After the Parade of Nations, a famous performer sings a beautiful song. It was written especially for the Olympics. Then there are more performances.

At the end of the opening ceremony, the Olympic fire is lit. And then, of course, there's the most spectacular show of **fireworks** I've ever seen. They fill the sky with colour for kilometres around.

After this memorable experience we go back to our rooms and begin to prepare for the hardest part – the competitions. While I'm walking to my room, I meet Estelle in the hall. It's easier for us to talk to each other now.

"Wasn't that incredible?" I say to her, still very excited.

"Yes. It was very special," she answers. "I was crying during the ceremony."

"Me too," I tell her. "But now the real competition begins. I'm very nervous," I say, honestly. "I mustn't make any mistakes."

"You're a great gymnast, Kate. You'll do very well. But I'm going to try to be even better than you," she says, competitively.

"Estelle, **whatever happens**, we can be friends now, I hope," I say softly.

"Maybe," she answers, and then she turns around and walks away.

CHAPTER 11 — The Big Day Arrives

Finally, the day of the Olympic gymnastics competitions arrives. In the end, Becky is competing too. Amanda, one of the girls in our team, fell and broke her leg, so Becky has got an opportunity to participate.

I don't sleep well the night before because I'm very nervous. Our last days of training were good but you can be easily disappointed in the real competition. It's so easy to make a mistake. You can suddenly forget the routine. You can lose your balance. Or worse, you can fall. All those years of training can be lost in a second.

We arrive at the stadium and enter from a back entrance, so at first I'm not prepared for the sight. The audience applauds loudly as we come out onto the **benches** and join the other competitors. I can't believe how many people there are. I've participated in many competitions before, but I've never seen an audience as large as this one. Gymnastics is one of the most popular spectator sports in the Summer Olympic Games.

The first gymnastics competitions are the team competitions. These determine which ones go to the finals. Five of the six gymnasts in each team compete and the top four results are counted. These competitions also determine which individual gymnasts advance to the finals. So I have to succeed both for my team and for myself.

It's much easier to do your routines if you're part of a team. I'm the third gymnast, so when it's my turn, I'm prepared and I do well. We all do well. In fact, we reach the finals. And, of course, so does the French team. Monique, Estelle's trainer, isn't there to support her, but Estelle is wonderful as usual. And, best of all, I also get to the individual finals.

The team finals are the next day. Eight teams are competing. For the final, each country chooses three gymnasts to represent it on each piece of apparatus. All three results are counted and the team with the highest results wins the gold medal. I'm chosen as one of the three gymnasts for our team. I'm the last one to perform. The two girls before me do a wonderful job. And now it's my turn. If I succeed, we can win. If I fail, we'll lose because of me.

I decide to take Andrew's advice. I just think of him and my parents and it works. In my mind, no one else is in the stadium and I'm just doing my routines for Andrew and my parents. I feel much stronger.

I start on the **vault**. It goes well, the same as it does in training. Then I go on the bars. In the middle I lose my balance a little and I hear the disappointment from the audience. I lose my confidence for a second, but it soon returns. My last routine is on the beam and that goes beautifully.

My last routine is on the beam and that goes beautifully.

After I finish, the French team comes on. Estelle is also third. The two girls before her do very well and the French spectators applaud loudly. Then Estelle comes out. Her routines are perfect. She doesn't do anything wrong.

I'm very worried. Our team might lose because of me. We wait impatiently for the results. Our entire team is holding hands. Ben and the other trainers are trying not to look too nervous.

After what seems like an eternity, the results finally appear in front of our eyes. The scores are very close, but there's only one winning team. My dream has come true – *we* are the winners of the Women's Gynmastics Team Finals!

I feel very proud as I stand on the Olympic winners' podium with the other members of my team. Our captain is given the gold medal and she holds it high for everyone to see. There is loud applause from the British spectators. We're all so happy.

The French team comes second. We all shake hands and talk about how close the competition was, but you can see how disappointed they are.

The competition isn't finished. Now the hardest part begins. I have to compete in the individual gymnastics competition and my greatest opponent is, of course, Estelle.

Estelle is first. She's absolutely brilliant. Monique chose some amazing music for her floor routine and **it really suits her**. She makes one small mistake on the bars, but she's a real professional and most of the spectators don't even notice. She finishes with a result of 37.087. You can't do much better than that. But I want to win, so I *have to* do better.

I watch each gymnast carefully and try even now to learn something to **improve** my routine. I'm the last gymnast. It's my turn. Estelle's result is still the highest. As we thought, the real competition is between Estelle and me.

The presenter calls my name: "And now Kate Armstrong from Great Britain."

I stand up and wait for a second. Then the music begins and I'm doing my routines. To tell you the truth, I don't remember anything of those crucial minutes of my life. I just do the best I can. I think about nothing.

I finish my routine and I go and sit down in my place. Ben comes to talk to me. I'm in my own world, far far away. I don't hear him. I just sit there and wait for the results.

The time passes very slowly. Every minute seems like an hour. Finally, we see the scores in front of us. Vault – 9.375, bar – 9.575 and floor – an incredible 9.712! That is a total of 38.387. "Wait a minute," I think to myself. "That's 1.3 points more than Estelle's final score." I can't believe my eyes. For a moment, I think I'm dreaming. But there's no mistake. The results are right there, before us. Suddenly, I feel a hand on my back and I immediately return to reality. It's Ben. "Congratulations, Kate!" he says, with an enormous smile on his face. "I knew you could do it." It's true. I've done it. I've won the gold medal!

Here I am on the podium again. I'm getting the gold medal. But this time I'm the only one. I listen to the British national **anthem**. They are playing it for me and only me. My parents and Andrew are sitting close to the podium and Andrew is shouting louder than everyone else. And then I look down and I see Estelle. Estelle's also standing on the podium, but below me. She's the silver medallist. She looks at me and smiles. And I think, "Estelle's a winner too, but this is *my* moment. *I* am the champion!"

This is my *moment.* I *am the champion!*

Questions on the Text

Chapter 1

1. Describe briefly Kate's daily routine.
2. What decision did Kate make about her training before she met Andrew? Why did she make this decision?
3. How did Kate's parents react to her news about her date with Andrew? What reasons did they give to justify their reaction?
4. How did Andrew influence Kate's future as a gymnast?

Chapter 2

1. What was Kate's dream before she went to the World Championships? Why did it change?
2. According to Kate, why did the French team win at the World Championships? Kate complimented Estelle. How did Estelle react to this?
3. What happened after the World Championships?
4. Describe the friendship between Kate and Becky.
5. Give two reasons why it's good for the athletes to train at Lilleshall.

Chapter 3

1. What information does Kate learn about Belarus from the Internet?
2. What was the British team's training routine in Belarus?
3. How did Kate's perception of herself change while she was at the training camp?
4. Describe Kate's relationship with the other girls in her team.

Chapter 4

1. Why hasn't Kate got a mobile phone with her?
2. What is the purpose of the medical examination?
3. What does Kate see on the roof? Why does it surprise her?
4. Becky describes two types of athletes. What are they and how do they differ?
5. In Kate's opinion, why does Monique come to talk to her?

Chapter 5

1. Some of the girls drank alcohol on the roof. What is a reasonable explanation for this?
2. Who accompanies Kate to the examination and why?
3. According to Kate, why are the Olympics different from other competitions?
4. Why does Becky feel frustrated?

Chapter 6

1. Ben comes to Kate's room looking very serious. What does she think has happened?
2. What bad news does Ben tell Kate?
3. Why is Kate surprised to hear the news? How does she try to explain it?
4. What does Kate try to hide from Ben in the beginning? Why does she do this?

Chapter 7

1. What stupid thing does Kate say to Becky?
2. What favour does Kate want from Estelle? What surprises Kate about Estelle's reaction to her request?
3. Why does Kate tell Andrew more than she told Ben?

Chapter 8

1. What does Kate begin to think about Ben?
2. According to Kate, Estelle might be responsible for her situation. Why does she think this?
3. What does Ben discover about the drugs in Kate's body?
4. Why does Kate begin to suspect Becky?
5. What does Kate learn from Andrew's phone call to Ben?

Chapter 9

1. How does Kate console herself?
2. Why did Estelle invite Monique to come up to the roof?
3. Who gave Kate the drugs and how?
4. What must Kate do before she can participate in the Olympic Games?
5. Why does Kate apologise to Estelle? What is important to Estelle?

Chapter 10

1. Describe briefly what happens at the beginning of the opening ceremony.
2. Who participates in the Parade of Nations and what is the role of the leaders?
3. The British delegation passes the audience. What happens at that moment?
4. How does the opening ceremony end?
5. Estelle is much friendlier to Kate now, but she's still extremely competitive. How do we know this?

Chapter 11

1. How does Becky get an opportunity to participate in the Olympic Games?
2. What two things do the results of the team competitions determine?
3. How do the Olympic officials choose the winners of the gold medal in the team competition?
4. What happens to Kate on the bars? How does she feel as a result of this?
5. What results do Kate and Estelle get in the individual competition? What does Kate think about Estelle?

English	Castellano	Català
advice	consejo	consell
afterwards	después	després
anthem	himno	himne
anything left	nada más	res més
as soon as	tan pronto como	tan aviat com
at least	al menos	almenys
aware	consciente	conscient
benches	asientos	seients
by this time	entonces	llavors
care	te preocupas	t'amoïnes
championships	campeonatos	campionats
change her mind	cambiar de opinión	canviar d'opinió
comb	me peino	em pentino
cool	fría	freda
costume	traje	vestit, roba
didn't complain	no se quejó	no es va queixar
disqualified	descalificada	desqualificada
do our best	hacerlo lo mejor que podamos	fer-ho el millor que puguem
either	tampoco	tampoc
even though	aunque	encara que
exciting	emocionante	emocionant
fall asleep	quedarme dormida	adormir-me
fireworks	fuegos artificiales	focs artificials

English	Euskara	Galego
advice	aholkua	consello
afterwards	ondoren	despois
anthem	ereserkia	himno
anything left	ezer gehiago	máis nada
as soon as	bezain azkar	tan axiña como
at least	gutxienez	cando / polo menos
aware	jakitun	consciente
benches	eserleku(ak)	asentos
by this time	ordurako	daquela, entón
care	arduratzen zara	preocúpaste
championships	txapelketa(k)	campionatos
change her mind	iritziz aldatzeko	mudar de opinión
comb	orraztu dut	peiteo
cool	hotza	fría
costume	jantzia	traxe
didn't complain	ez zen kexatu	non se queixou
disqualified	kanporatua	descualificada
do our best	ahal dugun hobekien egin behar dugu	facelo o mellor que poidamos
either	ezta ere	tampouco
even though	arren	aínda que
exciting	zirraragarria	emocionante
fall asleep	lo hartzen	ficar durmida
fireworks	su artifizial(ak)	fogos de luzaría

English	Castellano	Català
focus	concentrarse	concentrar-se
go on a date	tener una cita, salir	tenir una cita, sortir
hall	pasillo	passadís
hall of residence	residencia	residència
host	anfitrión	amfitrió
improve	mejorar	millorar
in line	de la fila	de la fila
instead	en su lugar	en el seu lloc
is beating	late	batega
it really suits her	le va realmente bien	li va realment bé
join	unirnos al	unir-nos a
jokes	chistes	acudits
knock on	llamo a	pico a
law	derecho	dret
let it show	dejar que se notara	deixar que es notés
official	representante	representant
ordinary teenager	chica corriente	noia normal
over there	allí	allà
parade	desfile	desfilada
performance	espectáculo	espectacle
releasing	liberando	alliberant
roof	azotea	terrat
routines	número, coreografía	número, coreografia
scores	puntuaciones	puntuacions

English	Euskara	Galego
focus	kontzentratzeko	concentrarse
go on a date	irten, gelditu	ter unha cita, saír
hall	korridore	corredor
hall of residence	egoitza	residencia
host	anfitrioi	anfitrión
improve	hobetzeko	mellorar
in line	ilarako	da ringleira
instead	bere ordez	no seu lugar
is beating	taupadaka	latexa
it really suits her	erabat ongi doakio	vaille realmente ben
join	bat egin	unirnos ao
jokes	txisteak	chistes
knock on	jo dut	peto na
law	zuzenbidea	dereito
let it show	nabaritu ... zedin	deixar que se notase
official	ordezkari	representante
ordinary teenager	neska arrunt	rapaza corrente
over there	han	alí
parade	desfile	desfile
performance	ikuskizuna	espectáculo
releasing	askatuz	liberando
roof	zabaltza	azotea
routines	saio(ak), koreografia	número, coreografía
scores	puntuazio(ak)	puntuacións

English	Castellano	Català
sensitive	sensible	sensible
shared	compartíamos	compartíem
succeed	tener éxito, hacerlo bien	tenir èxit, fer-ho bé
support	apoyo	suport
take back	retirar	retirar
team-mate	compañera de equipo	companya d'equip
top	mejores	millors
train	entreno	entreno
training	entrenamiento; prácticas	entrenament; pràctiques
tricked	tendiera una trampa a	parés una trampa a
trouble	aprieto, problema	compromís, problema
unfair	injusto	injust
vault	potro	salt de poltre
whatever happens	pase lo que pase	passi el que passi
winning	campeón	campió
yet	todavía	encara

English	Euskara	Galego
sensitive	sentibera	sensíbel
shared	banatzen genituen	compartiamos
succeed	arrakasta izaten	ter éxito, facelo ben
support	babes	apoio
take back	zuzendu	retirar
team-mate	talde-kidea	compañeira de equipo
top	onen(ak)	mellores
train	entrenatzen naiz	adestro
training	entrenamendu; praktikak	adestramento; prácticas
tricked	tranpa jarri zion	tendese unha trampa a
trouble	estutasun	aperto, problema
unfair	bidegabea	inxusto
vault	zaldia	poldro
whatever happens	zernahi gertatuta ere	sexa o que for
winning	txapeldun	campión
yet	oraindik	aínda